Bem-vindo! *(Welcome!)*

Retirement means it's time for a new adventure. And Portugal is a wonderful country that is full of rich history, stunning beaches and friendly people. These are just a few of the reasons retirees from around the world choose to call this part of the Iberian Peninsula home.

This journal can be the first step in making your retirement dreams a reality. Use these pages to capture all the adventures and challenges of your move.

Write out your answers to the questions and complete the activities. This will let you look back on all the details and feelings that may otherwise be forgotten over time.

Throughout this book, you'll also find interesting facts about Portugal and useful tips on making your new country feel like home. For example:

DID YOU KNOW?

There are almost 700,000 expats in Portugal. That's about 7% of the country's total population. New arrivals tend to gravitate to Portugal's bigger cities like Lisbon and Porto, or opt for the Algarve's beaches. But increasingly, more expats are discovering the charm and relaxed lifestyle to be had in smaller cities such as Coimbra and Braga.

Portugal is an exciting choice for retirees. You'll find it's easy to explore new interests while continuing the activities you find meaningful. Want to learn to surf? Travel with friends or volunteer? Do nothing but sip some ginjinha (cherry liquor) on your balcony? It's all possible.

What are the things that bring joy and purpose to your life now?:

DID YOU KNOW?

Portugal has the world's oldest bookstore. Established in 1732, Bertrand Bookstore in Lisbon's Chiado district is a must-visit when touring the city. It isn't difficult to spot - just keep an eye out for the gorgeous blue and white mosaic tiles (azulejos) decorating the exterior. Inside the shop, look for the art-adorned wall at the back dedicated to Portugal's most famous poet, Fernando Pessoa.

You're moving to Portugal! Hopefully you're looking forward to eating, and eating well. Fresh seafood, cheese and wine dominate Portuguese cuisine.

With Indian, Mediterranean, Moorish and South American influences, traditional cooking in Portugal showcases a wide range of flavors. In fact, some famous "Portuguese" dishes such as Cataplana (fish stew) originated elsewhere. And if you prefer meat instead of seafood, not to worry! Meaty options like as Arroz de Pato (duck rice) and Bitoque de Vaca (steak with fried egg) can be found everywhere.

When shopping for wine in Portugal, look for labels that include the DOC or DOP (Protected Designation of Origin) identification. This means the wine you're about to enjoy follows strict quality controls in order to guarantee authenticity.

PORTUGUESE
FOODS TO TRY

Francesinha: A hot sandwich with layers of toasted bread, meats, cheese and beer gravy.

Caracóis: Tiny snails in garlicky broth, eaten with toothpicks. Available May thru August.

Sardinhas Assadas: Whole sardines grilled over coals. Available March thru August.

Bola de Berlim: A sweet yeast donut loaded with fillings such as custard and Nutella.

Queijo da Serra: A soft sheep milk's cheese with an acidic flavor, from the Estrella Mountains.

Portuguese Word Puzzle

Test your knowledge with some common vocabulary. On the next page, find and circle Portuguese translations of English words. Some words, such as "total," have similar or identical spellings in both languages.

As a clue, the first letter of each Portuguese word is provided in parentheses **( )**. Answers run vertically, horizontally and diagonally. Solutions on pages 10 and 11.

1. Restaurant **(R)**

2. Hour **(H)**

3. Sorry **(D)**

4. Happiness **(F)**

5. Street **(R)**

6. Hot **(Q)**

7. Total **(T)**

8. Beach **(P)**

9. Airport **(A)**

10. Cold **(F)**

11. Wine **(V)**

12. Natural **(N)**

13. Today **(H)**

14. Week **(S)**

15. Minute **(M)**

16. Goodbye **(A)**

```
B U Q M J C F D N P C T S K R W
O S L Q Z D U M L X H O S D E O
L A Y D G B U E I E I L Y D S X
Z I B N K V V V I N H O A S T F
V M O O T X V B G T U D E E A P
F P M T O T A L G W I T R M U E
U W F D R W R P C C N L O A R C
L M Q W J K M U I V A R P N A I
H E Y W F T S L P B T L O A N P
H O J E R A E P V G U U R H T I
R M R C I F I U I C R E T L E W
F X A A O F N V S H A A O T F F
E E R K S K L E F T L D N T M J
C P E U S K D W S D D E M M B M
I O P S A B N X K F U U W Y J L
A Y N T V T Q W L Q H S Q J R S
```

1. Restaurant
Restaurante

2. Hour
Hora

3. Sorry
Desculpe

4. Happiness
Felicidade

5. Street
Rua

6. Hot
Quente

7. Total
Total

8. Beach
Praia

9. Airport
Aeroporto

10. Cold
Frio

11. Wine
Vinho

12. Natural
Natural

13. Today
Hoje

14. Week
Semana

15. Minute
Minuto

16. Goodbye
Adeus

```
B U Q M J C F D N P C T S K R W
O S L Q Z D U M L X H O S D E O
L A Y D G B U E I E I L Y D S X
Z I B N K V V V I N H O A S T F
V M O O T X V B G T U D E E A P
F P M T O T A L G W I T R M U E
U W F D R W R P C C N L O A R C
L M Q W J K M U I V A R P N A I
H E Y W F T S L P B T L O A N P
H O J E R A E P V G U U R H T I
R M R C I F I U I C R E T L E W
F X A A O F N V S H A A O T F F
E E R K S K L E F T L D N T M J
C P E U S K D W S D D E M M B M
I O P S A B N X K F U U W Y J L
A Y N T V T Q W L Q H S Q J R S
```

"Portugal has a peaceful feel about it. I sit on the terrace overlooking the vineyard there and I feel cut off from the world. You need that sort of thing."

-Sir Cliff Richard, renowned English musician

From attending opera at Lisbon's Teatro Nacional de São Carlos to relaxing near the crystal-clear waters of Dona Ana beach in Lagos, Portugal offers something for everyone.

What plans do you have for retirement that you can't do now?:

 **DID YOU KNOW?**

Forbes Magazine counts Portugal among the best places in the world for retirees to live, and ranks the Algarve region as one of the most desirable destinations for older adults.

Before your big move, read stories set in Portugal to help acquaint you with its culture, places and people. Compile a retirement reading list by filling in the blank books. If you're looking for recommendations, consider these titles:

The City and the Mountains, by Eça de Queirós. A satirical novel that compares the bleakness of upper-class life in Paris with the fulfillment found in the Portuguese countryside.

The Portuguese: A Modern History, by Barry Hatton. An entertaining tour through the history of one of the oldest countries in Europe.

Night Train to Lisbon, by Pascal Mercier. A fictional story focusing on the life of a Portuguese doctor during António de Oliveira Salazar's notorious dictatorship. An international bestseller that was made into a movie in 2013.

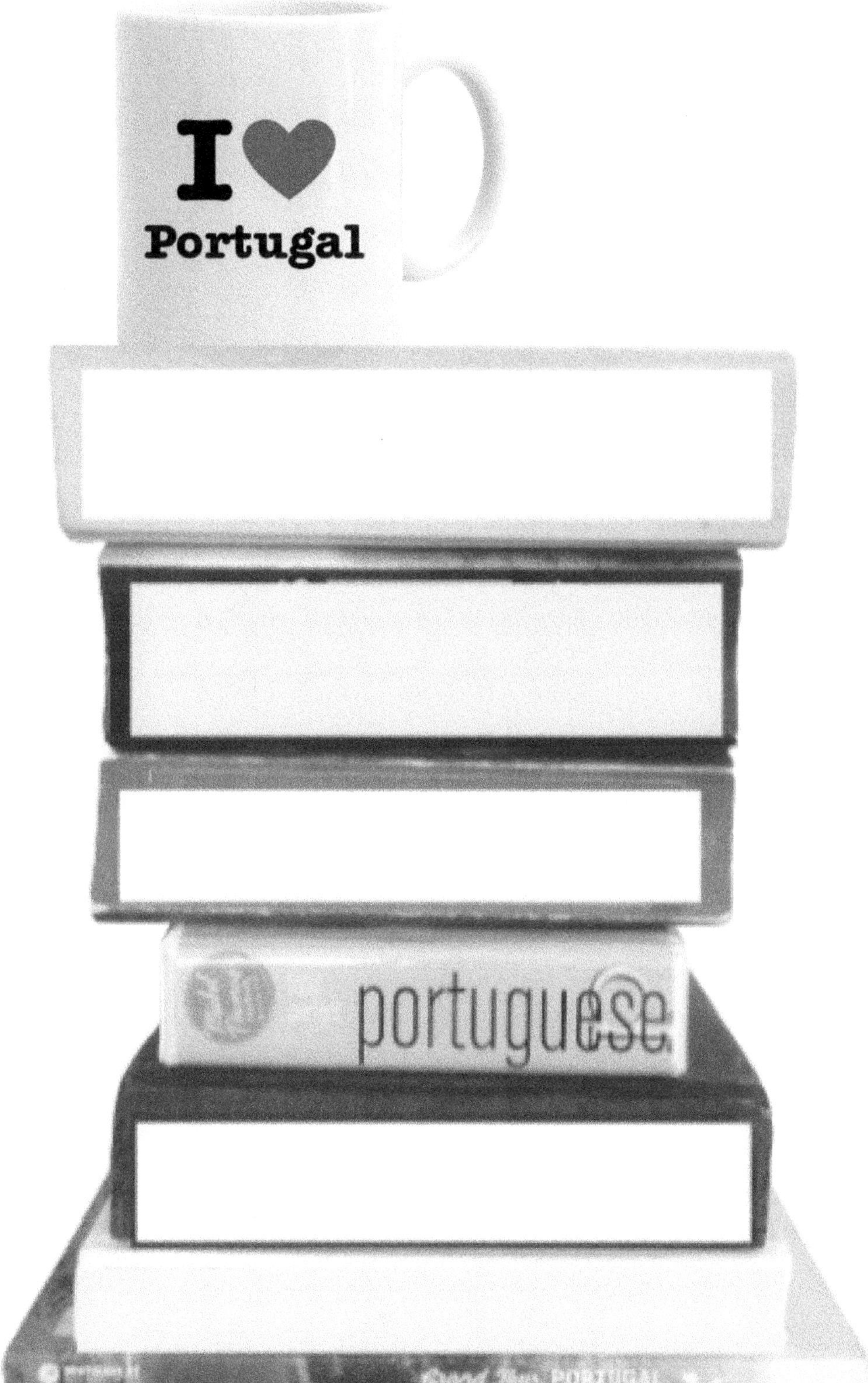
I
Portugal
portuguese
PORTUGAL

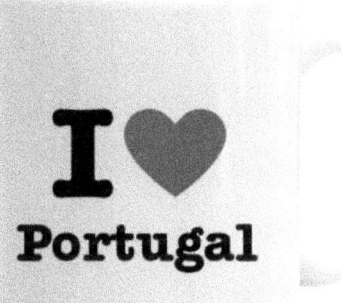

"If you can't figure out your purpose, figure out your passion. For your passion will lead you right into your purpose."

- Bishop T.D. Jakes
American preacher and author

Do you strive for calmness and peace in your life? Seek the thrill of adventure*? Or prioritize social connections? Perhaps all of the above.

Values are personal ideals that give our life meaning. They can affect how we navigate the opportunities and challenges of retirement.

*Portugal claims the world's longest suspension bridge. Pictured above, Bridge "Arouca 516" soars 175 metres over the Paiva river and links the two granite cliff faces on either side. eek!

Your set of personal values may include some of the following ideals. Circle the words that represent your passions, or write in your own.

altruism

religion

conservation

relationships

adventure

challenge

security

wellness

consistency

balance

knowledge

indepedence

fitness

generosity   joy

justice   fearlessness

acceptance   growth

exploration   spirituality

skill   adaptability

happiness _____

_____

An exercise called mind mapping can provide an excellent framework to visualize your values. Think of your three or four most important principles, and consider ways in which they might already be influencing your day-to-day life.

Moving to Portugal will require you to try new things and reach out to meet new people. It's the perfect opportunity to take stock of what is truly important in your life. And by fine-tuning your core interests and passions, you'll be well on your way to a retirement filled with meaning and purpose.

The mind mapping technique will help you create new value-centric ideas and also develop a plan of action around existing ones.

Using the thought cloud example diagrammed on Page 24, brainstorm and identify ways to have an exciting retirement that is authentic to you.

DID YOU KNOW?

A survey conducted by the expat-assistance company InterNations shows the top reasons people move abroad include: adventure, travel, quality of life, and language.

Will you have space in your new home for a furry friend, even on a temporary basis?

In addition to facilitating new friendships with other owners, research shows that pets can have a significant effect on the overall health and well-being of their human caretakers.

A study by Miami University Psychologist Allen McConnell shows that dog and cat owners have a greater level of happiness and experience less loneliness than those without animal companions. Pet owners also need to visit the doctor less often.

According to the study, these benefits may occur because pets give us a sense of meaning and belonging. Says McConnell, "You feel like you have greater control of your life."

Fostering a dog or cat is a wonderful way to experience the rewards of pet ownership without the long-term commitment. As with many countries, Portuguese animal shelters have limited space and rely on foster volunteers to provide care for homeless pets.

Shelters provide medical care and food for their animals living with fosters. All that volunteers are required to donate is their time! A list of Portugal's rescue associations by region can be found at www.adopta-me.org.

DID YOU KNOW?

Portugal is quite the dog-friendly country. Canine companions are welcome in many public spaces including cafes and restaurants (including some indoor ones) and designated beaches.

The rumors are true! Portugal offers many of the conveniences you may be accustomed to, such as (in no particular order):

 *High-quality healthcare*

 *World-class golf*

 *Organic and gluten-free food*

 *Cheap public transportation*

 *Grocery delivery services*

 *Michelin-starred restaurants*

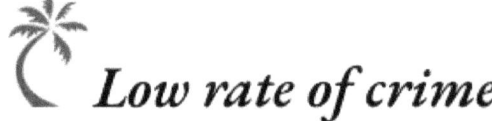 *Low rate of crime*

However, each major life change comes with its own unique challenges. Once the initial excitement fades, the differences you'll experience in Portugal may at first leave you feeling a bit off-balance.

It's normal to experience a sense of loneliness and unfamiliarity when moving somewhere new. According to a survey of 7,000 expats by HSBC Financial, it takes an average of eight months to feel settled in a new country. The same study cites "socializing with others" as a key factor in feeling at home.

TIP

To combat feeling adrift, develop a routine near your home for the first few weeks. By visiting the same local spots on a pre-planned schedule, your neighborhood will start to feel familiar. Some examples include a gym, restaurant, or your nearest library ("Biblioteca Municipal" in Portuguese).

When you move, what do you think you will miss most? Why?:

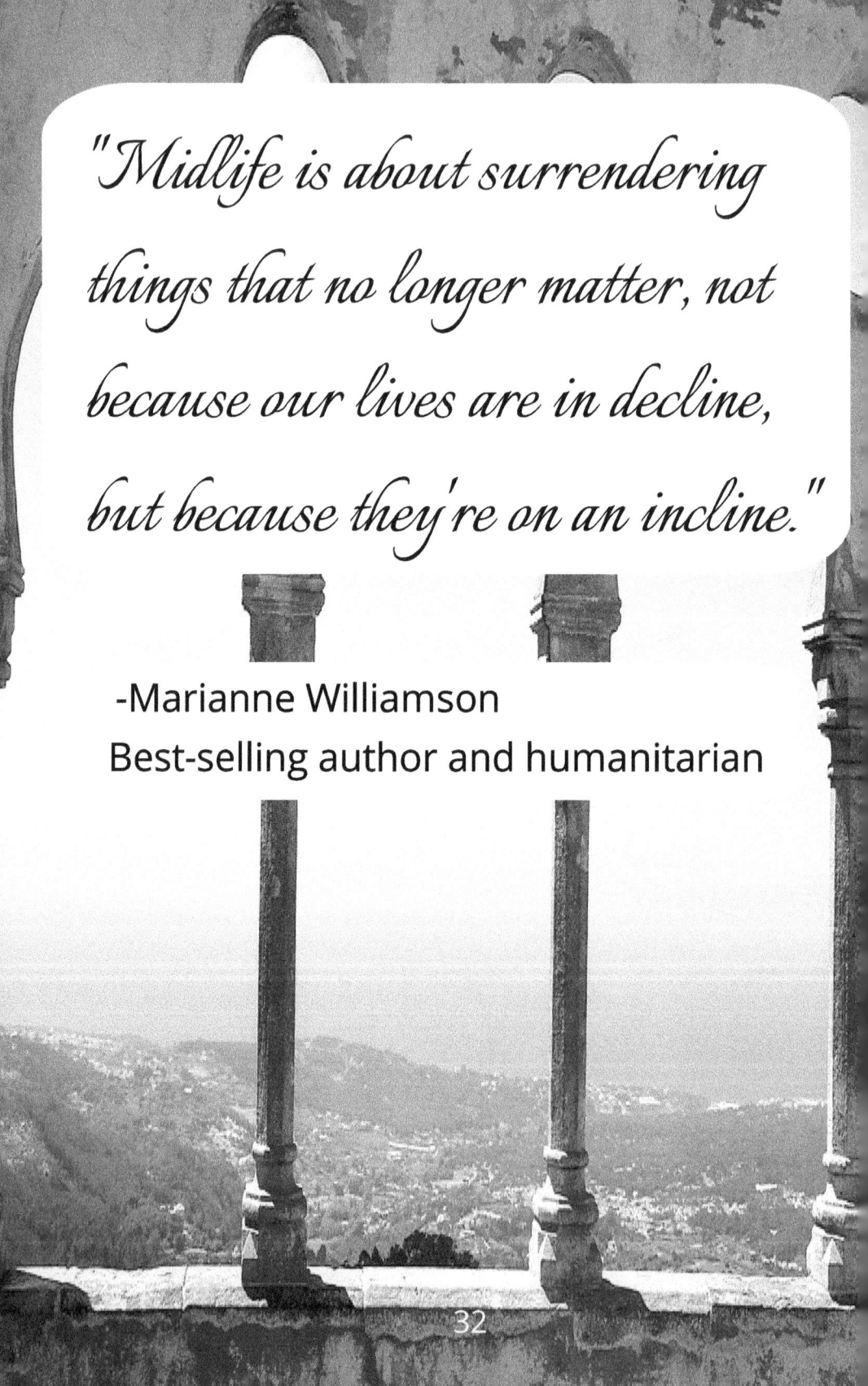

"Midlife is about surrendering things that no longer matter, not because our lives are in decline, but because they're on an incline."

-Marianne Williamson
Best-selling author and humanitarian

What is something you WON'T miss? Why?:

DID YOU KNOW?

Social media is a great way to connect with other expats, both before and after your move. For example, there are more than 100 various Facebook groups (both in English and Portuguese) dedicated to sharing advice and making the most of life in Portugal. With so much variety, you're sure to find a few groups that match your location and interests.

"Simplicity involves unburdening your life, and living more lightly with fewer distractions that interfere with a high quality life, as defined uniquely by each individual."

-Linda Breen Pierce
Award-winning author and public speaker

To prepare for retirement in a new country, experts recommend downsizing, then downsizing some more!

Take inventory of your belongings. Which of your possessions hold significant meaning, and which would be better left behind? The purpose of downsizing is to simplify your life. Try to adopt a "Take or Donate" mentality when sorting your stuff.

Go digital! Paper clutter can easily accumulate over the years. And many personal documents can be digitized then discarded. The same goes for photos and home movies. If you don't have the time to do it yourself, businesses such as legacybox.com and and securescan.com will do the task for you.

It's never too early to start clearing out clutter. Consider the 80/20 rule - research shows that we use only 20% of our belongings 80% of the time. Moving abroad is the perfect opportunity to live a fuller life with less.

Letting go of possessions can feel both liberating and daunting. If you would like some inspiration, Portugal expat groups on Facebook are full of members who relocated with only a few suitcases, and are glad they did!

DID YOU KNOW?

It is technically possible to use electronics and appliances from abroad in Portugal with the assistance of a voltage converter. Unfortunately, larger devices may blow a fuse in your home and will also have a reduced life expectancy.

Use the next pages as a starting point to determine the **non-negotiable** items you will take. To keep the list manageable, ask yourself questions such as, "is this easily replaced once I'm in Portugal?" The answer is often 'YES!'

TIP

Renting a long-term storage unit may sound tempting at first. But consider its monthly fee against the benefit of letting someone else appreciate your used furniture and household goods.

Must-Take to Portugal

Golf clubs—
much more
expensive
in Portugal
(example)

A bonus of retiring somewhere beautiful and relaxing like Portugal is that everyone you know will want to come visit!

Well, let's *assume* it's a bonus. You are of course allowed to tell people you're moving to Siberia, instead.

DID YOU KNOW?

Portugal boasts a whopping 300 days of sun annually. Outdoor pursuits such as hiking, boat trips, beach days and alfresco dining are available year-round. If winter activities are your preference, Portugal also has snow! Serra da Estrela is the highest mountain range in Portugal, where it snows from November to March.

How have your family and friends reacted to your upcoming move?:

Consider getting a VoIP (Voice over Internet Protocol) phone number. Using a VoIP will allow you to keep a phone number in your global area code of choice, and make keeping in touch with loved ones that much easier.

How many times have you thought to yourself that learning a new skill sounded interesting, but you didn't have the time to do it?

Maybe you are a budding shutterbug that looks forward to capturing nature, but could use a lesson in photography basics.

Or perhaps Portuguese fresh markets have you dreaming of cooking your own meals with local ingredients, but you struggle with new recipes.

According to the American Association of Retired Persons (AARP), the happiest retirees engage in three or more hobbies on a regular basis.

Companies such as Viator and Eventbrite provide a platform for local experts and instructors to offer a wide array of classes and workshops. Popular options in Lisbon and Porto include dancing, painting and photography.

Computer skills are particularly useful in retirement. Being able to make the most of your digital devices will allow you to easily keep in touch with family and friends when you move. You'll also have the know-how to take care of things like Portuguese banking and booking travel online.

The internet can give you access to advice, shopping, and community. Retirement is a terrific opportunity to grow your friend circle, and social media groups are especially valuable in finding folks with similar interests.

DID YOU KNOW?

Thanks to government support and a robust digital infrastructure, Portugal is one of Europe's fastest-growing tech hubs.

What new skills do you want to develop before moving to Portugal, or anticipate working on once you're there?

TIP

Internet-based education courses teach everything from foreign languages to woodworking to outdoor survival skills. Streaming services such as MasterClass, Skillshare and Craftsy are great places to explore curated lessons online.

Five Ways to Adjust to Life in Portugal

1. become a regular at your neighborhood café

2. start a new Facebook group for your specific hobby. - ie. "Poker Players in the Algarve"

3. join meetup.com

4. VOLUNTEER: RE-FOOD Portugal (fight hunger), REDE de Jovens para Igualdade (women's rights), Liga Contra o Cancro (against cancer)

5.

The first few days and weeks of your move to Portugal may feel oh-so busy, and perhaps even stressful. During this time of transition, you'll discover new culture, scenery, and of course, Portuguese food! Piri-piri chicken, anyone?

You may *also* experience Portugal's infamous bureaucracy. Don't say we didn't warn you! Tasks that might take a few minutes in more stream-lined countries may cost you hours of waiting and explanations in Portugal. Treat yourself to a glass of delightful vinho verde (literally "green wine") or a pastel de nata (a creamy custard pastry) afterwards. You will have earned it.

Even in offices, many people don't respond to emails or phone calls. It is often better to speak with someone in person, if you can. Keep in mind that most Portuguese businesses close for lunch.

Retiring and relocating to a new country are both life-changing events. What small steps can you take to make this transition more manageable?:

DID YOU KNOW?

It takes a native English speaker 600 hours, or 6 months of study, to become fluent in Portuguese. Eager to get started? It's possible to register for free language classes through your local Português Língua de Acolhimento (PLA).

"*Quem não arrisca não petisca*"

- Portuguese proverb

Translation: "Those who do not risk, do not have a snack." ie. to reap rewards, you first must be willing to take a chance.

Once you've arrived in Portugal and had some time to settle in, you'll reflect on your new experiences.

Think of two or three cultural differences you have already observed in Portugal - how did these make you feel?

Portugal has a relaxed approach to punctuality. While it is common to be five or ten minutes late to a social meet-up, running 30 minutes or more behind can make you appear inconsiderate.

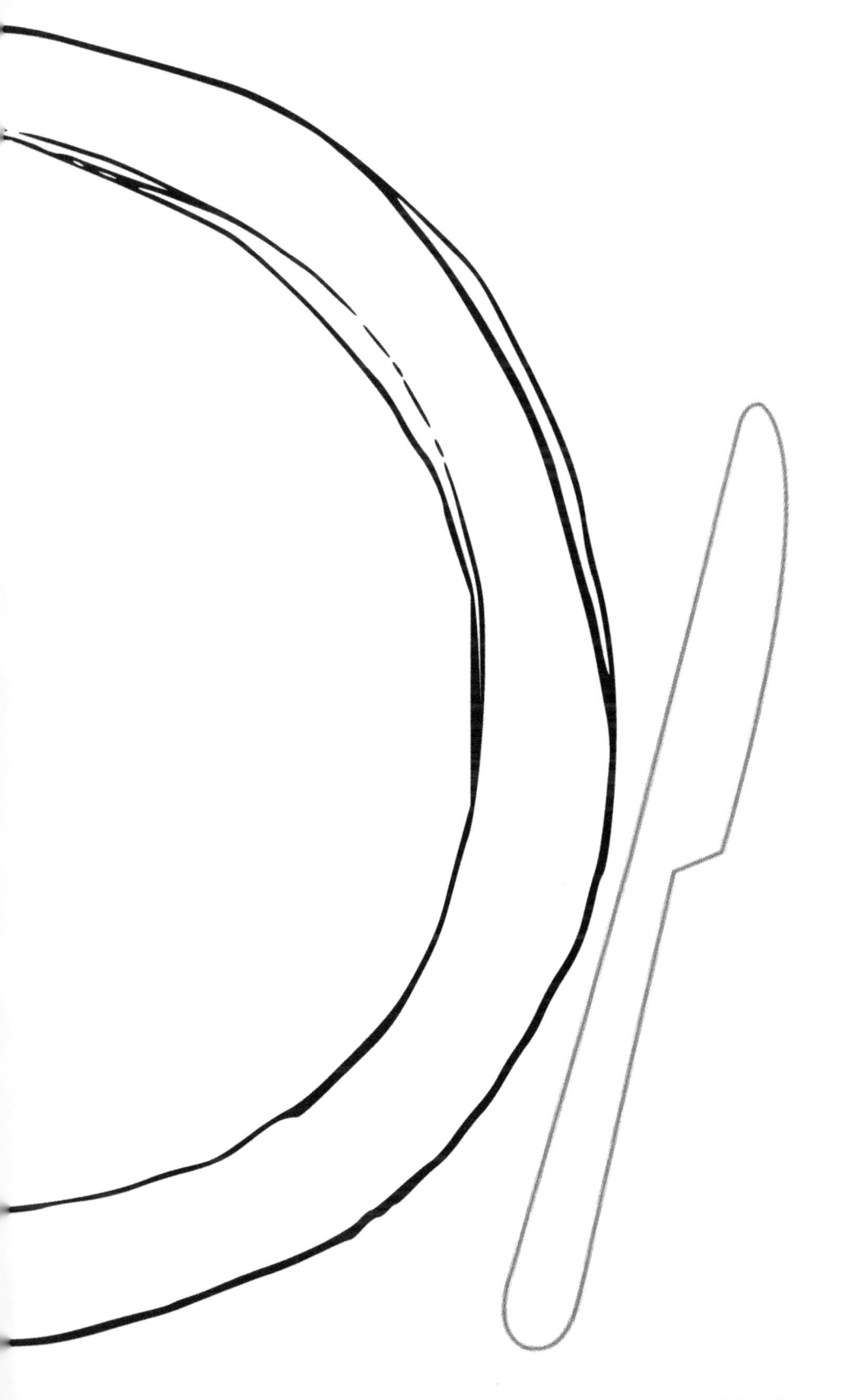

"*O que interessa é sentir o fado. Porque o fado não se canta, acontece. O fado sente-se, não se compreende, nem se explica.*"

-Amália Rodrigues
"Queen of Fado" and best-selling Portuguese artist in history

Translation: "What matters is feeling the fado. Because fado is not sung, it happens. Fado is felt, it is not understood, nor is it explained."

Popularized in the early 19th century, Fado is Portugal's dramatic, soulful music that is appreciated worldwide. Performers are accompanied by a Portuguese guitar while singing lyrics that describe homesickness and longing (or "saudade" in Portuguese). Fado literally translates to "destiny," and the haunting feeling of the music reflects this theme of fatalism. Want to experience it for yourself? In Lisbon, Casas de Fado ("Fado houses") are common in the Alfama and Bairro Alto neighborhoods.

DID YOU KNOW?

Fado was designated an Intangible Cultural Heritage of Humanity by UNESCO in 2011.

Have you learned anything about yourself since moving to Portugal? How has your worldview changed?:

DID YOU KNOW?

The national dish of Portugal is bacalhau, ie. dried and salted fish prepared in a variety of ways. Interestingly, the fish isn't native to Portugal; the cod used to prepare bacalhau is actually imported from Norway.

Below are some additional journal prompts to choose from. They relate to discovery, goals, and dealing with change, to help you make the most of your retirement in Portugal.

Which part of your move has surprised you the most?

How can you practice gratitude during this transition period?

If you haven't met locals yet, why do you think that is?

What are some ways you can give back to your new community?

Who made the most impact on you this week?

The last few pages have been left blank for you to treat this journal like a scrapbook.

Use the space to record the experiences of your first few weeks in Portugal in a tangible way.

Paste, staple or clip mementos like boarding passes and cultural event tickets to preserve memories that will bring a smile to your face when you revisit them.

Additional ideas include: temporary resident papers (once your official cards have arrived!), a photo of your first home in Portugal (even if it's an Airbnb), your first train card, etc.

Train travel within Portugal is managed by a single company: Comboios de Portugal. Booking your journey a week or more in advance can save you up to 50% off the price of your tickets!

www.ingramcontent.com/pod-product-compliance
Lightning Source LLC
LaVergne TN
LVHW061041070526
838201LV00073B/5133